What Is
Grace?

Basics of the Faith

Sean Michael Lucas, Series Editor

What Is Grace?

Sean Michael Lucas

P&R PUBLISHING
P.O. BOX 817 • PHILLIPSBURG • NEW JERSEY 08865-0817

Dedicated to Dr. George W. Robertson, senior minister at the First Presbyterian Church in Augusta, Georgia; preacher, model, lover of God's grace, friend.

Page design by Tobias Design

Printed in the United States of America

Library of Congress Cataloging-in-Publication Data

Lucas, Sean Michael, 1970-
  What is grace? / Sean Michael Lucas.
      p. cm. -- (Basics of the faith)
  Includes bibliographical references.
  ISBN 978-1-59638-211-4 (pbk.)
  1. Grace (Theology) 2. Reformed churches--Doctrines. I. Title.
  BT761.3.L83 2011
  234'.1--dc22
                                      2010054549

■ Grace is one of those words that people use with little understanding of what it means. I remember watching the ABC news coverage of former president Ronald Reagan's funeral. As his casket was wheeled onto the patio at his presidential library in Simi Valley, California, the Marine band began to play the hymn "Amazing Grace." News anchor Peter Jennings commented, "This song is so fitting for Reagan because it speaks of someone who was quite low and ends up achieving a great victory." For Jennings, *grace* meant the power and ability to succeed against the odds.

There are other examples of the way people misunderstand what grace is. On the Dave Matthews Band album *Big Whiskey and the GrooGrux King*, Matthews reflected his desire for New Orleans to recover from Hurricane Katrina by asking for grace and wondering when grace would return. Yet in published interviews he fully admitted that he didn't believe in God, going so far to claim that the idea of God is dead.[1] So the band's telling separated God from grace, which raised questions about the nature of this grace for which they pled.

For others, instead of separating God from grace, they simply believe that grace is about spiritual enlightenment, going with the fabric of the universe, or somehow having a general spirituality or religious sensibility. For example, the 1970s folk singer Judy Collins viewed grace this way: "We're always in the path of this power and my own feeling is that agnostics, atheists, spiritual people, and devoted churchgoers alike all have the same experience of grace because it is talking about forces unseen which are always around us."[2]

Such conceptions of grace—whether grace as moral uplift, grace apart from God, or grace as general spiritual enlightenment—are a long way from the biblical understanding. One of the key biblical statements on grace is found in Ephesians 2:1–10:

> And you were dead in the trespasses and sins in which you once walked, following the course of this world, following the prince of the power of the air, the spirit that is now at work in the sons of disobedience—among whom we all once lived in the passions of our flesh, carrying out the desires of the body and the mind, and were by nature children of wrath, like the rest of mankind. But God, being rich in mercy, because of the great love with which he loved us, even when we were dead in our trespasses, made us alive together with Christ—by grace you have been saved—and raised us up with him and seated us with him in the heavenly places in Christ Jesus, so that in the coming ages he might show the immeasurable riches of his grace in kindness toward us in Christ Jesus. For by grace you have been saved through faith. And this is not your own doing; it is the gift of God, not a result of works, so that no one may boast. For we are his workmanship, created in Christ Jesus for

good works, which God prepared beforehand, that we should walk in them.

Twice in this text, the apostle Paul declares that "by grace you have been saved" (Eph. 2:5, 8). Notice that this is not moral uplift; Paul says that it is by grace you *have been* (passive, something has happened to you) saved. Nor is it general spiritual enlightenment; this grace is specific activity directed toward particular people. In fact, according to the Bible, grace is more than good works or good karma, enlightenment or effort. It is more than that boost we need in order to do what we already know we ought to do.

Rather, the Bible declares that grace overturns a condition that is desperate. Ours is a condition of great bankruptcy, great ruin. Grace overturns our ruined condition in such a way that we are forced to confess that everything we have, everything that we are, every single blessing we've received, whether the reality of forgiveness and cleansing, hope and joy, worship and service—all of it is the result of God's grace.

Many of us think that grace is something we receive at the beginning of our spiritual journey. We start with grace, which saved "a wretch like me,"[3] but we move on in the Christian life by the strength of our own performance. However, what the apostle Paul wants us to understand, under the direction and guidance of the Holy Spirit, is that we are saved by grace, we are sanctified by grace, and we are glorified by grace. From beginning to end, it is all the result of the undeserved and uncoerced favor of God. As the eighteenth-century Welsh preacher, Thomas Charles of Bala, put it: "Not only is the foundation laid in mere grace, but the top-stone will be brought forth with shouting, 'Grace, grace!'"[4]

Why is this true? How can this be? What is it about experiencing God's undeserved, uncoerced favor that demands we live our entire lives, as Paul says in Ephesians 1:6, "to the praise of his glorious grace"?

RUIN OF OUR SIN

In order to understand the amazing character of God's grace, we must first understand the ruin caused by our sin. In the first three verses of Ephesians 2, the apostle Paul describes a universal condition. It is true of the newest newborn and it is true of the oldest person who has ever lived. This condition results from our sin and sinning. It is not only the result of original sin, but also our own actions of disobedience toward God that result in final spiritual death invading the present.

Spiritually Dead

In Ephesians 2:1, the apostle Paul notes, "you were dead in the trespasses and sins in which you once walked" (in the NIV, "in which you used to live"). In some ways it seems that Paul is saying something that is an apparent contradiction. How can someone be dead and yet very much alive? What is this condition of being dead in trespasses and sins? Paul is actually going to describe in a little bit more detail what this condition of "deadness" looks like in Ephesians 4:18–19. There Paul describes those who are not followers of God, those whom he characterizes as Gentiles. And he says that they "are darkened in their understanding, alienated from the life of God because of the ignorance that is in them, due to their hardness of hearts. They have become callous and have given themselves up to sensuality, greedy to practice every kind of impurity."

In light of Ephesians 4:18–19, what does it mean to be spiritually dead? Paul describes those who are spiritually dead in four ways. *First, those who are spiritually dead are those whose understanding is darkened*—spiritual realities for them do not compute. Their entire worldview is one in which the material, the sensual, represents the only reality there is. Only those things that their five senses can discern—what they can see, hear, touch, smell, or taste—are real. Such an understanding is a "closed box universe." There is no possibility of the supernatural, divine intervention, or holy beneficence. People who encounter life in terms of only what they can see have darkened understandings.

Second, those who are spiritually dead are those who are alienated from the life of God. They are alienated from new life, and that is the result of culpable ignorance. It's not as though there are those wandering around the world who say, "I wish I knew who God was. I wish I knew what God is like, but God hasn't shown me yet." No, Paul says that human ignorance is culpable and is the result of the hardness of our hearts. This is the condition that Paul describes as spiritual deadness—a darkened understanding, an alienation from God.

Third, those who are spiritually dead are callous. Not only is their understanding darkened, they are hardened to their condition. It doesn't bother them that they are alienated from God; it wouldn't occur to them that this would be a bad thing. *Fourth, they are ones who are greedy for sensuality*, eager to live for their basest desires, chained and enslaved to whatever their hungers dictate.

So those who are spiritually dead live with darkened minds and hardened hearts. It is important to recognize that this spiritual deadness is *caused* by trespasses and sins as well as *characterized* by them. Those who have darkened minds and hearts delight to live in the darkness. That's how it is possible for someone to be "dead in trespasses and sins" as well as "walk/live" in them. Those who are spiritually dead practice the dead deeds of their moral condition.

Morally Captive

It's not simply that mankind is not spiritually alive; rather, we are all actually captive. And in Ephesians 2:2–3, the apostle Paul describes this captivity in three ways. *First, he claims that we are morally captive to the course of this world.* Paul claims that "you were dead in the trespasses and sins in which you once walked, *following the course of this world.*" This language of "follow" is actually stronger. It is reminiscent of Romans 12:1, which the Phillips translation memorably rendered, "Don't let the world around you squeeze you into its mold." Those who are morally captive to the world are squeezed into the world's mold: they are forced into certain ways of thinking, believing, and acting, which represents the world's conventional wisdom.

D. Martyn Lloyd-Jones, in thinking about this text, put it this way: "They think as the world thinks. They take their opinions ready-made from their favorite newspaper, whether the left or the right. Their very appearance is controlled by the world and its changing fashions. They all conform; it must be done; they dare not disobey; they are afraid of the consequences."5 Now, that's not just some kind of abstract "they"; that's you and me. It is *our* culture, the conventional wisdom of our world, which squeezes us into its mold. If our culture claims that it is okay for a couple to divorce simply because they are unhappy, such wisdom squeezes us; it tempts us to trim the biblical message. If our world holds that painful slander is okay or "might makes right" politics is acceptable, such conventional wisdom squeezes us into its mold. If our world holds that sensuality—not just pornography, but flesh-driven sensuality—is *au currant*, then we feel pushed into its mold.

Second, not only are we morally captive to the course of this world, *we are morally captive to the devil himself*: "Following the course of this world, following the prince of the power of the air." Behind the apparent conventional wisdom of this world's age is the imperative force of the devil. I think we don't understand fully why Paul calls this usurper prince "the prince of the power of the air." It is clear that Paul has in mind spiritual reality, spiritual forces, cosmic powers that oppose the ways of God in this world. In Ephesians 6:12, Paul teaches that "we do not wrestle against flesh and blood, but against the rulers, against the authorities, against the cosmic powers over this present darkness, against the spiritual forces of evil in the heavenly places." Pitted against the ways of God, pitted against our Lord Jesus Christ, are spiritual forces headed by a usurper prince.

The way this usurper prince exercises his authority in the world is through "the spirit that is now at work in the sons of disobedience." That's how the devil works. He is not omnipresent. He is not able to be everywhere at once. Nevertheless, he is behind the conventional wisdom of this world that stands against the biblical wisdom of God. He is behind the spirit of this age, whether it is a spirit that tears down Christian religion, or whether it is a spirit that simply chips away and squeezes us into its mold.

Finally, Paul notes that we are not captive to the course of this world and to the devil, but *we are captive to our own disordered desires*. He observed in Ephesians 2:3: "among whom we all once lived in the passions of our flesh, carrying out the desires of the body and the mind." As we sin, some of us tell ourselves, "Well, I don't have to do thus and so. I'm free to walk away from that particular thing at any point and time. I can walk away from this particular sin. I can walk away from this particular habit anytime I want." Perhaps some have said that. Yet the fact of the matter is this: *we are not free not to sin*. And this is the case because we are morally captive to our disordered desires, to the passions of our flesh, to the passions of our body and mind.

Now what does that mean? It means when our disordered desires for stuff, whatever the stuff may be—the next electronic gadget, the next thing that will make us feel secure and significant—whenever that desire beckons, we are powerless. When sexual desires rise up, one finds oneself saying, "I can't fight against it." Perhaps for some it is the desire for food, drink, or alcohol. When those desires beckon, there is nothing to be done: you feel powerless before it. And even when one doesn't have opportunity to exercise bodily desires, the mind seems impossible to control. That's why Paul notes that those ruined by sin constantly are "carrying out the desires of the body and the mind."

This moral captivity is to an unholy trinity: the world, the flesh, and the devil. These forces are arrayed against us. And yet, it is not as though, in our condition of spiritual deadness, we fight against them. Rather, we welcome them—we gain pleasure from following the dictates and fashions of the world; we delight to please our own deceitful desires; and we willingly listen to the voice of the devil in the spirit of the age. In ways we cannot fully grasp, we are morally captive as a result of our sin.

Our Standing: Condemned

The apostle Paul tells us that we "were by nature children of wrath, like the rest of mankind" (Eph. 2:3). Now, this wrath of God is not like human wrath, some kind of anger that we can vent for a moment and then say, "Okay, I feel better now that I've gotten over that." Nor is it an anger like ours that seems somewhat irrational and uncontrollable. No, that's not what God is talking about here. The wrath of God is his righteous and just indignation against those who violate his ways and spurn his character.

Does that sound harsh? That is exactly what Paul describes. That is exactly our condition, those of us who have been ruined by sin. We were spiritually dead. We were made to be spiritually alive to God, to respond to him, to delight in him. But instead, we rebelled against him and experienced spiritual death. We were made to obey his law, to do what he calls us to do, to live in concert with his desires, but by our own sinful desires, we've spurned his way and have become morally captive. Even worse, we didn't obey the cosmic desires of God, but disobeyed and now are following the cosmic plan of the devil. It is only right for such a glorious being who sees his creatures acting in this way to bring his judgment.

Any parent whose child consistently spurns his character and commands would want to bring discipline. That is what we are called to do. But this discipline that God brings is not merely discipline for a moment. For those who are outside of Jesus Christ, who have experienced the ruin of our sin, it is eternal punishment; it is the expectation of the final judgment of death invading the present. That is what the writer of Hebrews claimed:

> For if we go on sinning deliberately after receiving the knowledge of the truth, there no longer remains a sacrifice for sins, but a fearful expectation of judgment, and a fury of fire that will consume the adversaries. . . . For we know him who said, "Vengeance is mine; I will repay." And again, "The Lord will judge his people." It is a fearful thing to fall into the hands of the living God. (Heb. 10:26–27, 30–31)

For those who are believers in Jesus Christ, this *was* our condition. But those who have not run to Jesus to plead his blood and righteousness find that this *is* their condition right now: a fearful expectation of judgment and fury of fire. If such a person were to die, they would fall into the hands of the living God and experience the vengeance of God.

Is it any wonder that Paul described the human condition as one in which we have been "ruined by our sin"? We know spiritual deadness, moral captivity, and divine condemnation. Such a condition is profoundly serious and not easily remedied. We wonder why God doesn't simply wipe away humankind right now in the light of our obstinate rebellion against him and his ways.

RICHES OF GOD'S GRACE

But the wonder of God's grace meets us right here: that though our sin and the act of sinning is deeply offensive to such a holy God, our God doesn't turn his back on us and walk away. Some of us as parents have gotten to the place where our children have so disregarded us that we have said, "Fine, if you are going to be that way, I'm going to walk away." We turn our backs on them. We may continue to pour out our indignation upon them, but we find no mercy for them. But, thankfully, God wasn't like us. He didn't turn his back on us. Instead, God does an amazing thing: he takes those ruined by sin and shows them undeserved, uncoerced favor.

In fact, the entire good news turns on two little words. They are found in Ephesians 2:4: "But God!"[6] Although we have been ruined by our sin, God in his mercy pours out the riches of his grace upon us in Jesus Christ. And he does it in such a way that he meets our need at every point and overturns our previous condition. He grants us new life and new sight, the very riches of heaven in Jesus Christ.

Spiritually Alive

First, the apostle Paul says that we were spiritually dead, but God made us alive with Christ (Eph. 2:5). Our under-standing had been darkened: we were unable to see and savor Jesus Christ. We could only see the material. We could only see the sensual. We could only evaluate things based on the conventional wisdom of this world. And the result was that we were alienated from God. Because our hearts were hard-ened by our own choices, we were callous and greedy for sensuality.

But God, in his undeserved, uncoerced favor, made us alive together with Christ. Those who are in Christ, who have trusted in Jesus Christ, who are united to Jesus Christ, they have been made alive with him. The apostle Paul puts it this way in 2 Corinthians 4:6: "For God, who said, 'Let light shine out of darkness,' has shone in our hearts to give the light of the knowledge of the glory of God in the face of Jesus Christ." We were blind, but now we see. We see the excellency of Jesus, his way of salvation, faith, and grace. Our hearts can no longer restrain themselves as we rejoice in the fact we were once dead, but now we are spiritually alive.

Morally Empowered

The apostle Paul says, "But God . . . made us alive together with Christ *and raised us up with him.*" We have experienced a resurrection. We were spiritually dead. We were morally captive. We were bound with the chains of the world, the devil, and our own desires. But now we are empowered. We are freed. In Romans 6:4 Paul noted that we have been raised with Christ so that "we might walk in newness of life." We can walk and live in new ways. While in the past we were not able not to sin, *now we are able not to sin.* By the power of God's Spirit, we are empowered to live in ways that please God. What does that look like?

Paul talks about it in Ephesians 4. There he describes this moral empowerment in terms of putting off the old self and putting on the new self. And then, beginning in Ephesians 4:25, he gets practical. Being empowered by God's grace means that we have power not to lie. We have power not to steal. We have power not to be bitter, not to harbor malice. We have power not to slander one another. We have power not to be sexually impure. We have power not to covet. We have power not to rebel against one another as couples, not to hate each other. We have power not to frustrate our children. We have power not to disappoint our employers or our employees.

Not only do we have power *not to sin*, but also for the very first time we have new power to live in ways that please God. We have power to tell the truth, not just in pressure situations, but to tell the very truths about our hearts. We have power to say what everyone already knows, namely that we are chief sinners, broken, and messy, that we are worse off than we think. We have power to be generous with others. We have a new power to forgive, to extend truly the forgiveness that Christ has shown us. Not only do we have power not to be sexually impure, we have power to be sexually pure, to cherish our bodies, to preserve sexual relations for marriage and for right uses in marriage. Now we have power to have a family and marriage that reflect our union with Christ and a relationship with our children that hopefully will foster faith in them. Grace doesn't simply affect "the hour we first believed";[7] grace affects and transforms everything.

Our Standing: Glorified

But God's grace doesn't stop there. Paul goes on to say that you were once condemned, but now you are glorified: "and raised us up with him and seated us with him in the heavenly places in Christ" (Eph. 2:6). In the past God looked at us through lenses of wrath, but now God looks at us in Jesus Christ. Now he sees us as beautiful and glorious, already seated with Jesus in his presence.

Paul noted this in Romans 8: "Those whom he predestined he also called, and those whom he called he also justified, and those whom he justified he also glorified" (8:30). This past tense language for glorified is important: for those who are united to Jesus Christ by faith, those who have been made alive and raised with him, God already sees

17

them as glorified. He already sees us sharing in the very glory of Christ. No longer does God view us as a judge would, but in Christ he views us as a loving father. Our standing has changed from condemned to glorified; such is the glorious result of God's grace: "There is therefore now no condemnation for those who are in Christ Jesus" (Rom. 8:1).

In the light of these glorious benefits, it is no wonder that the old slave-trader, John Newton, taught us to sing,

> Amazing grace—how sweet the sound—
> That saved a wretch like me!
> I was once lost, but now am found—
> Was blind, but now I see.[8]

We were wretches, ruined by sin, lost and blind. But God, out of his undeserved and uncoerced favor, poured out the riches of his grace upon us. Such grace should take our breath away and cause us to sing.

REASONS FOR GOD'S GRACE

And yet God's grace comes to us with a larger purpose. Notice that in the transition between Ephesians 2, verses 6 and 7, there's not a period, but a comma followed by a "so that." Paul writes, "But God, being rich in mercy, because of the great love with which he loved us, even when we were dead in our trespasses, made us alive together with Christ . . . raised us up with him and seated us with him . . . so that," for this purpose. Paul means to highlight the larger purpose of God's grace, the reasons God's grace comes to wretched, blind, lost, ruined sinners. What are the reasons God has for showing grace to us?

I would suggest that in Ephesians 2 Paul sets forward two reasons for God's grace. The first reason is that God desires us to *magnify* him. God's grace should cause us to worship him, to praise him, to glorify him. The second reason that God shows us his grace is that God has a *mission* for us. God has a cosmic mission and within this larger mission he has particular purposes for us to fulfill. To put it differently, grace transforms everything as we learn that we are loved not because we perform well or poorly, but because we are united to Jesus Christ. Empowered by this union with Jesus, we live new lives of worship and service as signs and agents of the new world to come.

Magnifying God

Notice how Paul, in giving us the reasons for God's grace, says that it is so that we might magnify God. Paul had already detailed this purpose three times in Ephesians 1. He notes that God's redemptive plan is "to the praise of his glorious grace" (1:6) and "to the praise of his glory" (1:12, 14). God's purpose is to be famous for his abundant, immeasurable, surpassing grace, and to be hallowed and vindicated before the nations and the spiritual forces that oppose him.

But in Ephesians 2:7 Paul explains this even more: "so that in the coming ages he might show the immeasurable riches of his grace in kindness toward us in Christ Jesus." It's as though throughout space and time, for all eternity, God desires to shine his spotlight upon his glorious grace shown to us in Christ Jesus our Lord in order that he might receive great glory and honor. God's purpose remains the same: that God might glorify God and enjoy himself forever as we glorify him and enjoy him forever. The constant refrain of Ezekiel puts it this way: "they shall know that I am the LORD" (Ezek. 5:13; 6:10; 7:27; 12:15; 28:22; 30:25; 34:27, 30; 39:6; 39:28).

Yet there are specific things that God desires to be highlighted, magnified, and worshipped. What are they? First, *God desires for his character to be magnified*. See how Paul does this. In Ephesians 2:4 he highlights the mercy and love of God: "But God, being rich in *mercy*, because of the great *love* with which he loved us." And in Ephesians 2:7 he focuses on the kindness of God: "so that in coming ages he might show the immeasurable riches of his grace in *kindness* toward us in Christ Jesus." These three words—mercy, kindness, and love—mutually reinforce one another in order to give to us a picture of the very character of God. In focusing on God's mercy, we see God's "overflowing active compassion"; highlighting his love, God moves toward us in steadfast love and commitment; naming his kindness, God shows his "sympathetic concern for our welfare."9 Thus, as God pours out his grace upon us, he rivets our attention on these aspects of his character: his compassion, loyalty, commitment, and concern.

Now, remember, this is the character of God as demonstrated toward us after we have been ruined by sin. We can't look at God's character and forget our ruin by our sin as described in Ephesians 2:1–3. We were spiritually dead. Our very understanding was darkened. We were culpably ignorant. Our hearts were hardened. We were greedy after all manner of sensuality. We were condemned. Every holy being in the world would run away from us, abandon us to our just deserts.

But God runs *toward* us, not away from us; he comes near us in Jesus Christ and saves us. Why does he do this? Not because we performed well and not because we are the beloved "problem child." No, God runs toward us because he is a God who is rich in mercy, great in love, overflowing in kindness toward us. What should our hearts do in response to such love, compassion, commitment, and concern? We should sing; we should rejoice; we should magnify the glorious grace of God.

Perhaps part of the reason some of us may struggle to praise and worship God—with our whole being, enlivened and passionate for God—is we don't really understand God's grace. And perhaps the reason we don't really understand God's grace is we fail to truly reckon with our ruin, who we are as sinners, our condition of spiritual deadness and moral captivity. Because if we really know who we are as sinners, if we really believe that we are far worse than we think, then we will look at God's grace and his character displayed in it, and we will sing:

> Father-like, he tends and spares us;
> Well our feeble frame he knows;
> In his hands he gently bears us
> Rescues us from all our foes
> Praise him . . .
> Widely as his mercy goes.[10]

As we reckon with this God, this God who pursued us all the way to the cross and the empty tomb in Jesus Christ, our hearts should say, "Lord, you have poured rich grace upon me. You are rich in mercy, great in love, full of compassion. Lord, it is overwhelming, your kindness. I revel in it and I sing your praise."

Not only does he call upon us to magnify God's character, he also calls us to *magnify God's son*. We caught this a little bit in the way Paul uses language in Ephesians 2:4–6. After all, it's by virtue of our union with Christ that the riches of God's grace come to us. But the way Paul expresses this is interesting. He actually makes up three words in verses 4–6; this is the only place they show up in the Greek New Testament. And these single words in the original language actually take several words to translate into English: "made us alive together with him" (*synzoopoieo*), "raised us up with him" (*synegerio*), and "seated us with him" (*synkathizo*). Why does Paul do this? He points out the riches of God's grace through and *with* (*syn* = with) the mediator, Jesus. The blessings of God's grace come through our union with Christ. As God sees us "with him," united to him, we are made alive, raised, and seated with Christ.

Moreover, Paul makes this same point in Ephesians 2:6, 7, and 10 when he explicitly uses the messianic name and puts the messianic name first: "seated us with him in the heavenly places *in Christ Jesus*"; "he might show the immeasurable riches of his grace in kindness toward us *in Christ Jesus*"; "we are his workmanship, created *in Christ Jesus* for good works." We tend to read over Christ Jesus or Jesus Christ as though they are exchangeable names. What Paul is saying is that these blessings come to us through the Messiah Jesus, through the promised one: the one who was the promised son of Isaiah 9; the promised branch of Isaiah 11; the promised suffering servant of Isaiah 53; the promised ruler who arrives upon a lowly donkey of Zechariah 9; the promised king who would be born in Bethlehem of Micah 5. All of God's grace comes to us through this promised Messiah, the one to whom the entire Old Testament testifies, *this Christ Jesus*.

Paul emphasizes this so that we might see the glories of Jesus. All the spiritual blessings we have come through and with Jesus. And yet, the greatest blessing that we receive through our union with Christ is not justification, not holiness, not glorification, not the spirit of adoption, not the spirit of prayer, not simply even the fact that God rejoices over us. Rather, *the greatest blessing we receive is Jesus*—that we are united to him and enjoy communion with the living God in and through him. *He* is our greatest blessing. *He* is our greatest delight.

The result of seeing Christ's glories in this way is that we long to sing and rejoice in him, we long to see and savor him as our great Savior and King. One of my favorite hymn texts is based on words by Samuel Rutherford, the seventeenth-century Scots Presbyterian divine, "The Sands of Time Are Sinking." As he suffered for preaching the gospel of grace, Rutherford was able to turn his eyes to Jesus to see and savor him:

> The King there in his beauty without a veil is seen;
> It were a well-spent journey though sev'n deaths lay
>   between:
> The Lamb with his fair army doth on Mount Zion stand,
> And glory, glory dwelleth in Emmanuel's land.
>
> The bride eyes not her garment, but her dear bride-
>   groom's face;
> I will not gaze at glory, but on my King of grace;
> Not at the crown he gifteth, but on his pierced hand:
> The Lamb is all the glory of Emmanuel's land.[11]

Christ the King is the glorious one for whom our hearts long. And God pours out the riches of his grace so that we might magnify God's own son.

In addition, God also desires us to *magnify his benefits*. Perhaps some of the most familiar verses in the Bible are Ephesians 2:8–9. We tend to focus upon "this is not your own doing . . . not a result of works" and perhaps may not reckon fully with "it is the gift of God." After all, to receive a gift is to receive grace. Whenever we receive a meal from someone, free tickets to a ball game, an anniversary present, or whatever it may be, we receive grace. And yet, in a far greater way, God grants us his benefits—being made alive with Christ, raised up with Christ, seated in heavenly places—as free gifts.

As a result, God calls upon us to magnify his benefits, to rejoice in the gifts that he has given us. Hence, it's right for us to think and talk about and to rejoice in justification. We should revel in the fact that we are as right with God as we will ever be because of the work that Christ has done on our behalf. We should rejoice in the purity that is already ours in Christ. We should rejoice in the fact that we are adopted sons and daughters, sons and daughters of the Living King. We should rejoice in the fact that he looks at us and sees us as glorious. It is right for us to rejoice and to magnify the benefits of the King.

Those of us who receive wonderful gifts at Christmas know what it is like to magnify these benefits, don't we? When we get a cool gadget or a precious bauble, we are eager to show it to others, to make much of it. In Christmas 2008 one precious gift I received was actually a family heirloom, an onyx ring with a diamond that was four generations old. I had previously thought we lost track of it and then discovered my parents had it. When my parents gave it to me at Christmas, I wanted to make much of the ring. Isn't it natural for those who are newly engaged to do the same? What do they do? The young ladies hold out their left hands for people to admire: "Oh look!" They make much of the ring; they make much of the gift.

We must see that to make much of the gift is actually to make much of the Giver. As we revel in the glorious gifts of God's grace, we actually are magnifying our God: that he is "good and forgiving, abounding in steadfast love" (Ps. 86:5). Far from making us arrogant or exclusive, boasting in ourselves as though we saved ourselves or made ourselves holy, such an understanding of God's grace drives us to make our boast in him. That's really the purpose of Paul's claim that "this is not your own doing . . . not a result of works." From the beginning of our salvation to the end, it is all of God's grace—he is the one who made us alive, raised us, seated us; he is the one who justified, sanctified, adopted, and glorified us; he is the one who sustains us, hears us, tends us, cares for us. And so, God calls upon us to boast in him and not to boast in ourselves. Paul says it this way in 1 Corinthians 1:30–31:

> Because of him you are in Christ Jesus, who became to us wisdom from God, righteousness and sanctification and redemption, so that, as it is written, "Let the one who boasts, boast in the Lord."

How this should humble us, that we who are ruined by sin might be given these riches, "such a great salvation" (Heb. 2:3)! Think of it—that we might know Jesus Christ who is beyond all beauty and all excellency. How this should humble us before God! How this should humble us before one another so that we would believe and live the reality that

"I'm not better than my brother and my brother is no better than me." Why? Because we come to the foot of the cross with the same ruined condition and we receive the same riches from the same storehouse, bought with the precious blood of Christ. How this grace should do away with rivalry and turf battles! Why? Because we come to the same Christ and we receive the same riches; our competency and sufficiency comes from God, not ourselves (2 Cor. 3:4–6). Oh, that we would be humbled before such a Glorious King who pours out his riches upon us! This should cause us to treat those who have sinned against us with mercy because God, who is rich with mercy, has been merciful to us. We should be moved to forgive "as God in Christ forgave you" (Eph. 4:32).

And how this grace should enliven our worship! Shouldn't such glorious riches give us a sense of holy joy in the very presence of the King as we worship together on the Lord's Day? The ordinary means of grace work because this God is so great and his grace is so rich. If this God doesn't look great, glorious, good, and gracious in our eyes, we can preach and we can do sacraments and we can do prayers, and it won't mean anything. But, if this God is this great, and this grace is this rich, then it should enliven our worship, and it should cause our hearts to run after God as we worship and praise him. Oh, that we would magnify this God so that his fame would run throughout the entire world, that all might know his glorious character, his beautiful Son, and his abundant benefits!

God's Mission

There is a second reason why God pours out his riches of grace upon us: he desires for us to join in his mission. In some ways, Ephesians 2:10 seems like a strange place to end this section. However, it fits with what Paul has been talking about to this point. In particular, Paul wants us to see that God's grace transforms us that we might serve as signs and agents of the new creation.

In saying that "we are his workmanship, created in Christ Jesus," Paul is telling us something very important that we may not have caught before. Paul is saying that we were originally created in Adam. In fact, he could have easily said, "we are his workmanship, created in Adam." We were originally created in Adam; if Adam, our representative head, had obeyed God in perpetual obedience, we would have known the blessing of God and been freed to do good works in Adam. However, Adam failed to obey God and the result was the story of Ephesians 2:1–3; we are ruined by our sin, plunged into a condition of sin and misery.

But now, for those united to Jesus, we are a new kind of "workmanship." Whereas in the past we were God's workmanship *created in Adam*, now we are God's workmanship *created in Christ Jesus*. As a result, we stand as those who are God's new creation. What is it that Paul said in 2 Corinthians 5:17? "If anyone is in Christ, he is a new creation. The old has passed away; behold, the new has come." It is the same thing here—we are a new creation, his workmanship created in Christ Jesus. What the new heavens and earth will be are foreshadowed in us. What the world will look like at the end of the age, when all will be put to rights again and all will be the way it ought to be, is being made manifest in us!

How much more grace can there be? Those of us in Adam who have experienced the pain, suffering, and brokenness of the old creation now know in Jesus the joy, healing, and righteousness of the new creation. Indeed, God looks at us and rejoices over us as signs of the new creation, God's workmanship created in Christ Jesus. Yet again, we are as signs and agents of the new creation called to enter into this world to do new works.

Paul is drawing a parallel in Ephesians 2:10 that we must notice. He observes that we are new creations, "created in Christ Jesus for good works . . . *that we should walk in them*." And this is in contrast to what we used to do in Ephesians 2:1–2: "you were dead in the trespasses and sins *in which you once walked*." This is the Adam/Christ parallel again: whereas, in Adam, we were "dead in trespasses and sins in which we once walked," now, in Christ, we are made alive in order to walk in the new works that God has prepared for us. You see, there is a difference; a new way of living is in play. Not only are we new creations, but there is also a new life that God has for us, a new way of being human.

And Paul describes that new way of being human in Ephesians 4:17–6:9. He tells us what it looks like to live out these new works that he has for us, this new way of living, so that we might demonstrate to a watching world what the new creation looks like. When we live faithfully together as families, as we honor one another as husband and wife, and as parents honor children and children honor parents, we demonstrate this new way of being human. As we work well for our employers, or as employers we care well for our employees, as we live lives in which we do not lie to others but tell the truth, as we forgive one another as Christ has forgiven us, we demonstrate that we are new creations. As we live lives of sexual purity, as we do not covet one another's things, as we do not slander one another, we display the new works of God. When we live in this world as free children of the great King, made alive with Christ and empowered by the resurrection, displaying for the world a picture of God's kingdom here and now, the world declares, "That's what the kingdom coming looks like. That's what the new creation looks like. There, in each one of these new believers who are new creations, this is what God's future looks like. Lord, I long for that."

What we must not miss is that as we do these new kinds of works empowered by God's Spirit and freed by God's grace, we are actually walking in step with the cosmic mission of God. This cosmic mission is not simply "me and Jesus," although that is important. We are not going to minimize a personal relationship with Jesus in the least. And yet, God saves us for a yet larger purpose that Paul describes in Ephesians 1:9–10:

> . . . making known to us the mystery of his will, according to his purpose, which he set forth in Christ as a plan for the fullness of time, to unite all things in him, things in heaven and things on earth.

What is God's cosmic purpose? To unite all things in Christ, things in heaven and things on the earth so that Christ will be all in all.

There is coming a day when Christ will fill all in all. At the end of the age, in the new heavens and new earth, we will enjoy the presence of God and Christ himself will be the light (Rev. 21:22–23). In the new heavens and new earth, all injustice will be set to rights; all death will be done away; sin will have no more dominion; and the creation itself will enjoy the freedom of the children of God. In the meantime, as we live in the light of who we are in Christ, as we live as new creations, as we live out these new works that God has prepared from the very foundation of the world, we serve as signs and agents of the end for which God created the world—Christ uniting all things in himself so that he might be all in all and all the world will glorify and enjoy him forever.

This means that God in his grace is fundamentally committed to overturning the evil and ugliness that sin has produced and restoring it to beauty. The lead singer from the rock band U2, Bono, has observed well that this is what makes grace different from karma. At the center of most religions is karma—"what you put out comes back to you." But at the center of Christianity is grace: "Along comes this idea called Grace to upend all that 'as you sow, so shall you reap' stuff. Grace defies reason and logic. Love interrupts, if you like, the consequences of your actions. . . . I'm holding out for Grace."[12]

Ultimately, that's what God's grace does. In his undeserved and uncoerced favor, God takes us, ruined and ugly, and he turns us into beautiful beings, new creations. He pours out the riches of his grace upon us through and with Jesus Christ, and he calls us into the world to live in new and different ways, so that the entire world might in the end bow their knee to King Jesus and say, "I praise this King because, by his grace, he makes beauty out of ugly things." And all this is to the praise of his glorious grace—thanks be to God!

NOTES

1. http://www.rollingstone.com/news/story/28600068/dave_matthews _shares_the_stories_behind_big_whiskey_and_the_groogrux_king/3.
2. These first paragraphs borrow from Sean Michael Lucas, *On Being Presbyterian: Our Beliefs, Practices, and Stories* (Phillipsburg, NJ: P&R, 2006),

33–34. The Judy Collins quote is from Steve Turner, *Amazing Grace: The Story of America's Most Beloved Song* (New York: HarperCollins, 2002), 217–18.

3. "Amazing Grace." Words: John Newton, 1779. Music arranged by Edwin O. Excell.

4. Edward Morgan, ed., *Thomas Charles' Spiritual Counsels* (Banner of Truth, 1993), 14. See Zechariah 4:7.

5. D. Martyn Lloyd-Jones, *God's Way of Reconciliation: Studies in Ephesians 2* (Grand Rapids: Baker, 1972), 21–22.

6. James M. Boice, *Ephesians* (Grand Rapids: Baker, 1997), 51.

7. "Amazing Grace." Newton and Excell.

8. Ibid.

9. Andrew Lincoln, *Ephesians*, Word Biblical Commentary (Dallas: Word, 1993), 100, 110.

10. "Praise, My Soul, the King of Heaven." Words: Henry F. Lyte, 1834. Music: Sir John Goss, 1869.

11. "The Sands of Time Are Sinking." Words: Anne R. Cousin, 1857. Music: arr. Edward F. Rimbault, 1867.

12. Michka Assayas, *Bono: In Conversation with Michka Assayas* (New York: Riverhead, 2005), 203–4.